mal ha favourites

Rohani Jelani

Delicious hawker recipes from the crossroads of Asia—including Malaysia's most famous dishes like Penang Fried Kway Teow, Banana Fritters and Asam Laksa.

PERIPLUS

Ask any true-blue Malaysian living or studying abroad what he misses most about home and chances are he'll blurt out fried *kway teow*, *rojak* or *roti canai*! These are not dishes lovingly prepared by doting mothers or aunts in home kitchens but affordable, hearty fare dished up by hawkers trading from simple stalls.

These hawker stalls may be set up under a shady tree on a street corner or clustered in rows in open-style coffee shops. Customers perch on plastic stools around Formica-topped tables, which they share with fellow diners and everyone is happy to tuck in, oblivious to heat and discomfort. Yet, despite these less than perfect surroundings and the often dubious hygiene standards, the crowds faithfully return, again and again, because they deem good food far more important than immaculate tables or air-conditioning.

Hawker food is something almost every Malaysian grows up with. Which child does not remember watching mesmerized, as the *roti canai* (pancake) man effortlessly and miraculously tosses and twirls his dough in the air until it is paper thin? And who can ever forget the mouth-watering aroma of chilli and garlic being noisily stir-fried in a cast iron wok for Penang-style fried *kway teow* (flat rice noodles)?

Hawker food is so good and cheap, one wonders why anyone would bother cooking it at home? Well, not everyone has the good fortune to be living close to a really good hawker stall. So, if you want to eat prawn noodles or *mee goreng*, (fried noodles) you may just have to make it yourself. And with reliable recipes such as the ones presented in this book, you can.

The recipes for the hawker dishes featured here stick fairly closely to the ones you might eat at regular hawker stalls. However, knowing that they will be used in a home kitchen, we have taken a couple of liberties. We have, for example, made more liberal use of vegetables, meat and seafood, ingredients normally used with caution by stall holders, in an effort to keep prices low. And our recipes are lower in fat than those from the stalls. We have also modified some recipe methods to ensure that they work in a domestic kitchen. We hope this will help you serve authentic yet healthy hawker favourites to your family and friends.

Coconut milk (*santan*): To obtain fresh thick coconut milk, add 125 ml ($^1/_2$ cup) water to the grated flesh of one coconut and squeeze. To obtain fresh thin coconut milk, squeeze the grated flesh with another 625 ml ($2^1/_2$ cups) water. Powdered coconut milk is readily available in most supermarkets.

Flour: Various types of flour are used in Malaysian hawker dishes, most notably plain flour (*tepung gandum*), cornflour (*tepung jagung*), rice flour (*tepung beras*) and tapioca flour (*tepung ubi*). All are available from Asian food stores.

Palm sugar (*gula Melaka*): Made from either the aren or coconut palm, this raw sugar has a slightly smoky flavour. Substitute with soft brown sugar.

Jicama (*bangkuang*): Also known as yam bean, jicama is a tuber with a beige skin and crisp white interior.

Noodles (*mee*): Of the many types of noodles used in Malaysian hawker dishes, the following are featured in this book: fresh yellow egg and wheat-flour noodles (*mee*), dried rice-flour vermicelli (*meehoon*), fresh flat rice-flour noodles (*kway teow*), fresh round rice-flour noodles (*laksa* noodles), mung bean-flour glass (or cellophane) noodles (*tung hoon*).

Pandan leaf (*daun pandan*): Also known as screwpine leaf, pandan (or pandanus) leaves are used to add fragrance to savoury dishes, and green colour to sweet dishes. May be substituted with vanilla essence but the flavour will be different.

Peanuts, toasted (*kacang goreng*): Place peanuts in a saucepan or wok and fry over low heat for 15 to 20 minutes, stirring constantly to prevent burning. When crisp and cooked, remove from heat and set aside to cool. Rub the nuts with your fingers to dislodge the papery skins. To separate the skins, place nuts on a tray and toss gently—as you do this, the skin and nuts will gather themselves into separate piles, making it easy for you to discard the skins.

Prawn paste (*hae ko*): Completely unrelated to shrimp paste (*belachan*), prawn paste is a black treacly seasoning.

Shrimp paste (*belachan*): Dried shrimp paste is usually sold as a crumbly pink to brown block which must be toasted before cooking. Either wrap in foil and roast, dry fry in a pan, or toast above a gas flame on the back of a spoon.

Yam (*ubi keladi*): Also known as taro, this oval, starchy tuber with dark brown skin, and flesh ranging from white to purple, must be thickly peeled and cooked thoroughly as undercooked taro can cause irritations in the throat and mouth.

Basic Chilli Sauce

4 fresh red chillies, sliced
2 cloves garlic, roughly
  chopped
2 tablespoons sugar
2 tablespoons white
  vinegar
$1/_2$ teaspoon salt
2 tablespoons tomato
  ketchup
5 tablespoons water

For chilli sauce to accompany prawn fritters (page 6) and fried spring rolls (page 8), combine all the ingredients and blend until smooth. For chilli sauce to accompany savoury yam cake (page 12), omit the tomato ketchup and add another 2 tablespoons of water to the mixture, then blend.

Chicken Rice Chilli Sauce

4 red chillies, chopped
2 cloves garlic, chopped
3 cm ($1 1/_4$ in) young
  ginger, chopped
$1 1/_2$ tablespoons calamansi lime juice (*limau
  kasturi*)
1 tablespoon sugar
$1/_2$ teaspoon salt
5 tablespoons chicken
  stock or water

Pound or blend all the ingredients and use as an accompaniment to chicken rice (page 44).

Seasoned Sliced Chillies

10–15 bird's eye chillies,
  finely sliced
2 tablespoons light soy
  sauce
2 tablespoons fresh lime
  juice

Combine the chillies, soy sauce and lime juice in a small bowl and use as an accompaniment to claypot chicken rice (page 42). When serving with Cantonese noodles (page 34) or glass noodles and fishball soup (page 21), omit the lime juice.

Prawn Paste Dip (*Hae Ko*)

2 tablespoons prawn
  paste (*hae ko*)
2 tablespoons hot water

Combine the *hae ko* and water and use as an accompaniment to spicy tamarind laksa (page 25).

Fragrant Shrimp Paste Dip (*Sambal Belachan*)

3 red chillies, chopped
3 teaspoons crumbled
  roasted shrimp paste
  (*belachan*)
1 teaspoon sugar
1/4 teaspoon salt
1 tablespoon lime juice

Slice the chillies and pound finely in a mortar and pestle with the crumbled shrimp paste. Add the sugar, salt and lime juice, mixing well with the stone pestle, and use as an accompaniment to Hokkien noodles (page 37).

Pink Pickled Onion

2 medium purple onions,
  peeled and halved
  lengthways, thinly sliced
3–4 tablespoons white
  vinegar
4 teaspoons sugar
Red colouring (optional)

Place onions in a bowl with vinegar and sugar. Set aside for 1 hour before serving as an accompaniment to *murtabak* (page 52). Commercial pickled onion is always tinted a bright shade of red or pink. If you wish to duplicate this look, add a drop of red colouring into the liquid.

Chicken Stock

1 chicken carcass or 500 g
  (1 lb) chicken bones
4 slices ginger
10 peppercorns
2 litres (8 cups) water

Rinse chicken carcass or bones thoroughly, discarding any blood clots and fat. Place in a roomy saucepan and add ginger slices, peppercorns and water. Bring to a boil, skimming off any scum that rises. Allow stock to simmer on low heat for 1 hour, until the liquid is reduced to roughly 1 litre (4 cups). Strain and discard the solids. Used in Cantonese noodles (page 34) and Hainanese roast chicken rice (page 44).

Crisp Fried Shallots

6–8 shallots, peeled and
  thinly sliced
125 ml (1/2 cup) oil

Heat oil in a frying pan or wok over medium heat and fry the sliced shallots until golden brown, taking great care not to over-brown them as this makes them taste bitter. Carefully remove fried shallots with a slotted spoon, transferring them onto a plate lined with paper towels. If not using them immediately, store in a dry, airtight jar to preserve their crispness.

Prawn Fritters (Cucur Udang)

200 g (1 1/2 cups) plain flour
1/2 teaspoon baking powder
1/4 teaspoon ground turmeric
1 level teaspoon salt
250 ml (1 cup) water
100 g (1/2 cup) Chinese chives, trimmed and cut into 4-cm (1 1/2-in) lengths
100 g (2 cups) bean sprouts, rinsed
Oil for frying
20 medium prawns, peeled, with tails intact

Serves 4
Preparation time: **20 mins**
Cooking time: **30 mins**

1 Sift flour, baking powder, tumeric and salt into a mixing bowl and add the water, mixing with a spoon to make a fairly thick batter. Stir in the chives and bean sprouts.

2 Locate a suitable ladle that is not too large or too deep, about 5 to 6 cm (2 in) across. Ensure that it has a heatproof handle.

3 Heat oil in a small saucepan up to a depth of 4 cm (1 1/2 in) over medium heat. Place ladle in the oil to heat it. After 4 to 5 minutes, lift the now hot ladle from the oil, allowing excess oil to drip off.

4 Spoon in enough batter to fill the ladle almost to the top. Press a couple of prawns into the top of the batter and gently lower the ladle into the oil. After 2 to 3 minutes, when the base of the fritter has formed a crust, gently prise it out of the ladle with the tip of a spatula or small knife and allow it to continue frying in the oil until golden brown all over. Refill the ladle with more batter and continue until all the batter is used up.

5 Drain fritters on absorbent kitchen paper. Cool for 5 to 10 minutes before cutting fritters into cubes or slices. Serve with basic chilli sauce (see page 4).

Press one or two prawns into the batter in the ladle, then lower carefully into the oil.

Prise out fritter from ladle using a spatula and allow it to continue cooking in the oil.

Fried Spring Rolls (Popiah)

2 tablespoons oil
4 cloves garlic, finely chopped
100 g ($^1/_2$ cup) peeled prawns or skinned chicken breast, diced
1 500-g (1-lb) jicama (*bangkuang*), peeled and finely shredded to yield $4^1/_2$ cups
1 100-g ($3^1/_2$-oz) carrot, peeled and finely shredded
10 french beans, topped and tailed and thinly sliced on an angle
150 g ($1^3/_4$ cups) finely shredded cabbage
1 teaspoon sugar
$^1/_2$ teaspoon salt
$^1/_4$ teaspoon ground white pepper
2 teaspoons cornflour
20 sheets frozen or fresh spring roll skins
500 ml (2 cups) oil for deep frying

Sealing paste
3 tablespoons plain flour
2 tablespoons water

Serves 4
Preparation time: 1 hour
Cooking time: 30 mins

1 Heat oil in a roomy frying pan or wok and fry garlic until golden brown. Add prawns (or chicken), fry for 1 to 2 minutes until firm, then add cut vegetables. Stir-fry over medium heat until vegetables are wilted, about 10 minutes. If the mixture seems wet, increase the heat and stir fry until the excess moisture is gone.
2 Season with sugar, salt and pepper. Spread the vegetable mixture in an even layer and sift the cornflour over the mixture. Toss and stir until well combined. (The filling should be quite dry—a filling that is too moist will cause tears in the spring roll skins.) Transfer filling onto a shallow plate and leave to cool.
3 Separate spring roll skins but keep them covered with a damp but well wrung cloth to prevent the skins from becoming dry and brittle.
4 Make a sealing paste by mixing the flour with just enough water to form a thick, gum-like paste.
5 Lay spring roll skin on a clean, dry working surface, with one corner pointing towards you. Place a spoonful of filling roughly one-third way up from the base of the spring roll skin. Fold the bottom third of the spring rolls skin over the filling to enclose it and then fold sides down neatly. Now roll tightly, brushing a little of the flour paste around the edges to seal the spring roll. Form all rolls this way until filling is used up. Lay rolls neatly on a tray and cover with cling film or a clean cloth. (Spring rolls can be made several hours ahead and kept refrigerated.)
6 Close to serving time, heat oil in a saucepan or wok. Fry spring rolls over low heat until golden brown, 10 to 15 minutes (if the oil is too hot, the skins will be rough and blistered). Drain on absorbent paper and serve hot, accompanied by basic chilli sauce (see page 4).

Place filling one-third up from the base of the skin and fold the skin to enclose the filling.

Fold the sides down neatly then roll it up, using a little sealing paste to seal the roll.

Banana Fritters

10–12 cooking bananas such as *pisang raja* or *abu*
Oil for deep frying

Batter
100 g ($^3/_4$ cup) rice flour
50 g ($^1/_3$ cup) flour
$^1/_2$ teaspoon salt
$^1/_2$ teaspoon sugar
160 ml ($^2/_3$ cup) water

1 To make the Batter, combine rice flour and flour in a small mixing bowl; stir in the salt and sugar. Add all but 2 tablespoons of the water. Stir until free from lumps; the Batter should coat the back of a spoon thinly (add more water if needed).
2 Peel the bananas and slice each in half lengthwise.
3 Pour the oil into a pan or wok to a depth of 3 cm (1 in) and heat over medium heat.
4 Working with a few pieces at a time, dip banana slices into the Batter to coat thoroughly and then gently lower into the hot oil.
5 Fry bananas until golden brown on both sides. Remove from the hot oil with a slotted spoon. Drain on paper towels and serve warm.

Potato or yam fritters can be made from this recipe also. Peel 2 small sweet potatoes or 1 medium yam and cut into $^1/_2$-cm ($^1/_4$-in) slices. Dip in the batter used in the recipe above and deep-fry in hot oil until golden brown.

Serves 4
Preparation time: **20 mins**
Cooking time: **20 mins**

Savoury Yam Cake

1 small yam (taro), about 400 g (13 oz), peeled and cut in 1 cm (¹/₂ in) cubes, to yield 2 cups
3 tablespoons oil
4 shallots, chopped
1 tablespoon dried prawns, soaked
¹/₂ teaspoon salt
¹/₂ teaspoon Chinese five-spice powder
¹/₄ teaspoon ground white pepper
100 g (²/₃ cup) rice flour
3 tablespoons tapioca or cornflour
1 level teaspoon salt
550 ml (scant 2¹/₄ cups) water
¹/₄ teaspoon alkali water

Garnish
3 tablespoons crisp fried shallots
3 tablespoons finely sliced spring onions (scallions)

1 Place yam cubes in a heatproof container and steam for 20 minutes, or until tender. Set aside.

2 Heat oil in a frying pan or wok and fry chopped shallots over medium heat until just beginning to brown. Add drained prawns, fry for 2 to 3 minutes before adding yam cubes. Stir-fry for 2 more minutes, then season with salt, five-spice powder and ground pepper. Turn off the heat.

3 Combine rice flour, tapioca flour and salt in a pan with water, mixing well until mixture is smooth and completely free from lumps. Add the alkali water.

4 Put pan on low heat, stirring continuously with a wooden spoon. As the mixture heats up, it will start to thicken. When it reaches the consistency of a thin custard, immediately take the pan off the heat and add the prepared yam. Stir until well combined.

5 Transfer yam cake mixture into a 22-cm (9-in) round or square heatproof glass dish or metal cake tin. Place in a steamer over rapidly boiling water and steam for 25 to 30 minutes. Turn off heat and remove cake from steamer tray. Allow it to cool completely, then cut into 4-cm (1¹/₂-in) squares.

6 Garnish with fried shallots and spring onion. Serve with basic chilli sauce (see page 4).

Serves 4
Preparation time: **30 mins**
Cooking time: **40 mins**

Peel and cube the yam (taro).

Stir-fry the yam cubes with onions, prawns, salt, five-spice powder and pepper.

When the flour mixture thickens, remove from heat and add in the fried yam cubes.

Steam the yam cake for 25 to 30 minutes.

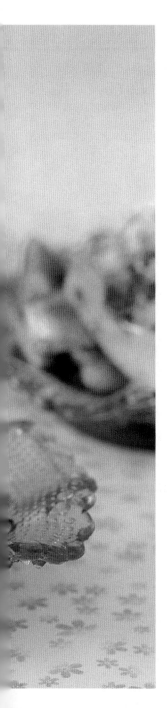

Fruit Rojak

1 small jicama (*bangkuang*)
$^1/_2$ small cucumber
$^1/_4$ firm unripe (green) papaya, peeled
$^1/_2$ medium green guava or 4 small water apples
  (*jambu air*)
1 small unripe green mango, peeled, or
  1 Granny Smith apple
$^1/_4$ ripe pineapple, peeled
100 g ($^3/_4$ cup) toasted peanuts (see page 3),
  finely crushed

Sauce
3–4 large red chillies
2 teaspoons crumbled, roasted shrimp paste (*belachan*)
1 rounded tablespoon tamarind paste soaked in
  5 tablespoons water
$3^1/_2$ tablespoons prawn paste (*hae ko*)
5–7 tablespoons sugar

1 Roll cut the jicama, cucumber, papaya and guava
(slice diagonally, then rotate fruit before slicing again
to ensure uneven pieces). Cut pineapple into wedges
and slice 1 cm ($^1/_2$ in) thick. If using water apples,
cut into thick wedges.
2 To prepare the sauce, finely pound chillies and
roasted shrimp paste together in a mortar and pestle.
(The number of chillies you use depends on how hot
you prefer your rojak to be.)
3 Squeeze, stir and strain the tamarind to obtain
tamarind juice and combine it with the pounded
chillies and shrimp paste, prawn paste and sugar. Stir
until well mixed.
4 Toss fruit, sauce and half the peanuts together in a
mixing bowl. Transfer into a serving dish or individual
bowls and sprinkle the top with the rest of the crushed
peanuts. Serve immediately.

Serves 4
Preparation time: **30 mins**
Assembling time: **5 mins**

Place the fish in the centre of a banana leaf.

Fold the banana leaf into a long packet and secure the ends with toothpicks.

Pan-fried Fish wrapped in Banana Leaf
(Ikan Panggang)

500 g (1 lb) fish steaks
or small whole fish
1–2 banana leaves for
wrapping

Marinade
2 rounded teaspoons
tamarind pulp
60 ml ($^1/_4$ cup) water
2 teaspoons salt
2 level teaspoons chilli
powder
2 teaspoons curry
powder
2 teaspoons turmeric
powder

Dip
2 rounded teaspoons
tamarind pulp
125 ml ($^1/_2$ cup) water
2 red chillies, roughly
sliced
4 bird's eye chillies,
roughly sliced
3 shallots, peeled and
roughly sliced
1 clove garlic, peeled and
roughly sliced
2 teaspoons crumbled,
toasted shrimp paste
(*belachan*)
$^1/_2$ teaspoon salt
2 level teaspoons sugar
1 tablespoon freshly
squeezed lime juice

1 To prepare the marinade, first extract the tamarind juice. Stir tamarind pulp in the water, squeeze and strain. In a small bowl, combine the tamarind juice with the salt, chilli, curry and turmeric powders. Spread this mixture over the fish and set aside for 20 minutes (no longer than that as the acid in the tamarind will start to 'cook' the fish).

2 While waiting for the fish to marinate, prepare the dip. Prepare tamarind juice (follow the same procedure as earlier) and combine it with the rest of the dip ingredients. Whisk for a few seconds in a blender or food processor until the mixture is smooth.

3 Wrap fish in banana leaves, securing the ends with toothpicks. Heat 3 tablespoons oil in a large frying pan and pan-fry the fish over medium heat for 6 to 8 minutes on either side (depending on the size and thickness of the fish). To test if cooked, pierce the thickest part of the fish with the tip of a knife—it should flake easily and be opaque in colour. If the flesh is translucent, cook it for a few more minutes.

4 To serve, place in banana leaf packets on a serving dish and unwrap fish at the table. Serve with the dip.

Use either fish steaks, small whole fish (ikan kembung or ikan selar), or slices of skate/sting ray (ikan pari) or red snapper (ikan merah). Gut and clean fish, rinse off any traces of blood and pat dry with paper towels. Small fish should be left whole, but make 2 to 3 shallow diagonal cuts on each side to allow marinade to penetrate and to ensure even cooking. If using fish steaks, they should be cut into slices $1^1/_2$–2 cm ($^3/_4$ in) thick. These should only be given a very brief rinse and then pat dry with paper towels.

Serves 4
Preparation time: **30 mins**
Standing time: **20 mins**
Cooking time: **20 mins**

Mutton Soup (Sup Kambing)

Sup kambing sold at hawker stalls generally does not include carrots and potatoes but we add it to our version to make the soup tastier and more substantial.

3 tablespoons oil
4 cm (1$^1/_2$ in) cinnamon
4 cardamoms
4 cloves
1 star anise
2 tablespoons plain flour
600 g (1 lb 3 oz) mutton
  or lamb on the bone
  (either from the ribs,
  shoulder or shin)
2 large or 4 medium
  tomatoes, cut in wedges
1$^1/_2$ litres (6 cups) water
1 small carrot, sliced
1 medium potato, peeled
  and cubed
1 medium onion, cut into
  thin wedges
Salt to taste
2–3 tablespoons crisp
  fried shallots
2–3 tablespoons sliced
  celery leaves (*daun sup*)

Spice mix
2 tablespoons coriander
  seeds
1 teaspoon white
  peppercorns
1 tablespoon cumin seeds
5 shallots, thickly sliced
5 cloves garlic, thickly
  sliced
4 cm (1$^1/_2$ in) ginger,
  thickly sliced
1 red chilli, cut into 2-cm
  ($^3/_4$-in) lengths
5–7 tablespoons water
$^1/_2$ teaspoon ground
  turmeric

1 To prepare the spice mix, place coriander and peppercorns in a small pan over low heat and roast until fragrant, about 3 minutes, stirring constantly. Add the cumin seeds and roast for another 2 minutes. Cool slightly before grinding finely in a mortar and pestle or an electric grinder. Place shallots, garlic, ginger and chilli in an electric blender. Add just enough water (about 5 to 7 tablespoons) to allow the blades to grind the mixture finely. Transfer to a bowl and mix in the ground spices and turmeric. Set aside.

2 Heat oil in a pan and fry the whole spices for half a minute before adding the spice mix. Fry over low heat until mixture begins to brown and oil separates. Dust in the flour and stir to make a smooth paste.

3 Cut mutton or lamb into 4-cm (1$^1/_2$-in) pieces and remove any visible fat. Place meat in the pan and, when it starts to brown around the edges, add tomatoes. Cook for 5 minutes until tomatoes start to soften, then pour in the water and bring to a boil.

4 Reduce heat to low and simmer for 1 to 1$^1/_2$ hours or until meat is tender, adding another 500 ml (2 cups) water if the soup seems too thick.

5 Add all the vegetables, salt to taste and cook for another 15 minutes or until vegetables are tender.

6 Ladle soup into individual bowls and serve hot, garnished with a spoonful of fried shallots and sliced celery leaves.

Serves 4
Preparation time: **30 mins**
Cooking time: **2 hours**

Glass Noodles and Fishball Soup

2 tablespoons oil
4 cloves garlic, bruised
4 slices ginger
100 g (1¹/₂ cups) dried whitebait (*ikan bilis*), briefly rinsed in a sieve
1¹/₂ litres (6 cups) water
200 g (6¹/₂ oz) glass noodles (*tung hoon*) or 500 g (1 lb) fresh rice noodles (*kway teow*)
200 g (4 cups) bean sprouts
20 fish balls (see recipe below, or store bought)
Salt and pepper to taste
4 tablespoons crisp fried shallots to garnish
1 cup finely shredded lettuce to garnish

Fishballs
4 tablespoons water
¹/₂ teaspoon salt
¹/₄ teaspoon ground white pepper
300 g (10 oz) mackerel (*tenggiri papan*), skinned and boned to yield 160 g (5¹/₂ oz) flesh only
4 teaspoon cornflour

Serves 4
Preparation time: 30 mins
Cooking time:
  1 hour 20 mins

1 If making homemade fishballs, combine the water, salt, pepper and cornflour in a small bowl, stirring well until salt dissolves and there are no lumps of dry cornflour. Cut fish into small pieces and place in the a food processor. Process the fish finely, adding the cornflour mixture a little at a time until it is a smooth, tacky paste.

2 Put a small pan of lightly salted water to boil. Using two wet teaspoons, form the fish paste into small balls roughly 2 cm (³/₄ in) across and drop them into the boiling water. As they float to the top, remove with a slotted spoon. Continue making the fishballs this way until all the paste is used up. Yields 25 to 30 balls.

3 To make the soup, heat oil in a roomy saucepan and fry the garlic and ginger until fragrant, about 1 minute. Add prepared whitebait and fry for 2 to 3 minutes until fragrant and beginning to brown.

4 Add water, bring mixture to a boil and lower heat. Simmer stock over low heat for 40 to 60 minutes. Strain stock into a clean pan and discard solids.

5 Prepare glass noodles by blanching in a pan of boiling water for about 3 minutes. Drain in a colander. Fresh rice noodles (*kway teow*) will need only 2 minutes blanching; drain in a colander.

6 Blanch bean sprouts for 30 seconds, drain and refresh by running tap water over them for 1 to 2 minutes. Drain well.

7 When ready to serve, reheat the stock, add the fishballs and cook for 2 to 3 minutes. Season to taste with salt and pepper.

8 Divide noodles and bean sprouts between 4 deep serving bowls. Ladle on the soup and fishballs and garnish with fried shallots and shredded lettuce. Serve immediately, accompanied with seasoned sliced chillies (page 4).

Prawn Noodles Soup

3 tablespoons oil
450 g (1 lb) prawns, peeled and deveined, tails intact (reserve heads and shells)
5 cloves garlic, chopped
1 tablespoon sugar
2 litres (8 cups) water
2 chicken thighs or drumsticks
150 g (5 oz) dried rice vermicelli, blanched for 2 minutes
225 g (8 oz) fresh wheat noodles, blanched for 2 minutes
225 g (4 cups) bean sprouts, blanched for 2 minutes
225 g (4$^1/_2$ cups) kangkong, (water spinach) or, blanched,
2 hard-boiled eggs, peeled and quartered
3 tablespoons crisp fried shallots (see page 5)

Chilli Paste
12–15 dried chillies, cut in lengths, soaked and drained
2 fresh chillies
1 teaspoon dried shrimp paste (belachan), toasted and crumbed
5 shallots, roughly chopped
3–4 tablespoons oil
$^1/_4$ teaspoon salt
1 teaspoon sugar

1 Heat oil in a wok over high heat and add the prawns. Stir-fry until prawns are firm and pink. Remove from the wok and set aside.

2 Add the chopped garlic to the wok and stir-fry until golden brown. Add the reserved prawn shells and heads and stir-fry over high heat for 5 to 6 minutes. Sprinkle in the sugar and fry for 2 more minutes.

3 Pour in the water and bring to a boil. Reduce heat to low and cook for 30 to 40 minutes. Add chicken thighs to the stock and simmer for 20 minutes until chicken is cooked. Take wok off the heat. Remove chicken, place on a plate and set aside to cool before stripping off the skin and shredding the meat, discarding the bones. Set aside.

4 While the prawn stock is simmering, prepare the chilli paste. In a blender, finely grind the dried and fresh chillies, shrimp paste and shallots, adding a little water if necessary. Heat oil in a wok and fry the ground Chilli Paste over low heat until the mixture is thick and oil separates. Add salt and sugar and remove pan from the heat. Transfer to a small serving bowl.

5 Allow the stock to cool and strain stock into a clean pan. You should have about 1$^1/_2$ litres (6 cups) prawn broth. Taste and adjust seasonings as necessary by adding salt, pepper or a touch of sugar. Bring to a boil again just before serving.

6 To serve, place a portion of rice vermicelli or wheat noodles, vegetables, prawns, shredded chicken, water convolvulus and eggs in a deep soup bowl. Ladle on the hot broth, sprinkle on a generous spoonful of fried shallots and serve immediately. Serve the Chilli Paste separately in a small sauce dish.

Serves 4
Preparation time: **40 mins**
Cooking time: **1$^1/_2$ hours**

Spicy Tamarind Laksa (Asam Laksa)

1 lb (450 g) mackerel or red snapper, cleaned
1 in (2¹/₂ cm) fresh ginger, grated
2 slices dried garcinia fruit (*asam gelugor*)
1 teaspoon salt
1¹/₂ litres (6 cups) water
2 torch ginger buds (*bunga kantan*), quartered lengthwise
5 sprigs Vietnamese mint (*daun kesum*)
2 teaspoons salt
3 tablespoons sugar
300 g (10 oz) dried laksa noodles or 450 g (1 lb) fresh laksa noodles

Spice Mixture
15 dried chillies, soaked in warm water for 20 minutes and chopped
4 fresh chillies, chopped
8 shallots, chopped
2 stalks lemon grass, bottom 10 cm (4 in) only, thickly sliced
2 teaspoons dried shrimp paste (*belachan*), toasted and crumbled

Garnish
1 small cucumber, cut into matchstick pieces
200 g (1 cup) fresh pineapple, cut into matchstick pieces
1 shallot, thinly sliced
1 torch ginger bud (*bunga kantan*), thinly sliced
40 g (1 cup) mint leaves
1 red chilli, thinly sliced

1 Place fish, ginger, garcinia slices and salt into a pan and cover with 1 litre (4 cups) water. Bring to a boil and reduce heat to low. Cover pan and poach fish until cooked, about 15 minutes. Remove pan from heat. When the fish is cool enough to handle, remove from poaching liquid and remove bones. Set aside. Strain fish stock and discard bones, reserving the stock.
2 To make the Spice Mixture, place dried and fresh chillies, shallots, lemon grass and shrimp paste in a blender and add enough water to grind until smooth.
3 Place Spice Mixture into a large pan and add reserved fish stock and the remaining 500 ml (2 cups) water. Add the torch ginger buds, mint, salt and sugar. Bring to a boil, reduce heat to low, and cook for 30 minutes. Add the fish and cook another 15 minutes. Taste and adjust seasonings.
4 Bring a large pan of water to a boil and cook the dried laksa noodles for 5 to 7 minutes or until tender. If using fresh laksa noodles, blanch in hot water for 1 to 2 minutes. Drain noodles in a colander and run tap water over them to remove excess starch. Drain well before transferring to a serving dish.
5 To serve, place a portion of noodles in a deep bowl and ladle in the fish broth. Top with the cucumber and pineapple, shallot, torch ginger slices, mint leaves and chillies and serve with prawn paste dip (*hae ko*) (see page 4).

Serves 4
Preparation time: **40 mins**
Cooking time: **1 hour 45 mins**

Curry Laksa

5 tablespoons oil
5 cm (2 in) cinnamon
1 sprig curry leaves
650 g (1¼ lb) chicken pieces on the bone, skinned and cut into bite-sized pieces
2 stalks lemon grass, bottom 10 cm (4 in) only, bruised
1 litre (4 cups) water
1 teaspoon sugar
2 teaspoons salt
10 long beans, cut into 3-cm (1¼-in) lengths
10 pieces fried tofu balls (*tofu pok*), sliced 1 cm (½ in) thick
300 ml (1¼ cups) thick coconut milk
300 g (10 oz) fresh yellow noodles
100 g (3¼ oz) dried rice vermicelli (*meehoon*)
500 g (10 cups) bean sprouts
4 tablespoons crisp fried shallots, optional
4 calamansi limes, halved

Spice paste
2 onions or 8 shallots, chopped
5 cloves garlic, chopped
3 red chillies, sliced
1 teaspoon shrimp paste (*belachan*), crumbled
250 ml (1 cup) water
5 tablespoons meat curry powder

1 To make the spice paste, blend onions, garlic, chillies, shrimp paste and water until fine. Transfer to a bowl and stir in the curry powder to make a paste.

2 Heat oil in a roomy saucepan and add the cinnamon and curry leaves, frying for a few seconds until fragrant. Add the spice paste and cook on low heat, stirring constantly, until mixture is well cooked and oil separates, about 15 minutes.

3 Add chicken and lemon grass and cook on medium heat until chicken pieces are firm, 15 to 20 minutes.

4 Pour in the water and bring to a boil. Reduce heat, add sugar and salt and simmer for 15 minutes before adding the long beans, sliced tofu balls and coconut milk. Simmer for another 10 minutes before switching off the heat.

5 Meanwhile, put a large pan of water to boil and blanch the rice vermicelli (3 minutes), bean sprouts (30 seconds) and the yellow noodles (2 minutes). Drain well in separate colanders.

6 To serve, place a portion of blanched *meehoon*, yellow noodles and bean sprouts in a deep serving bowl and ladle on a generous helping of curry gravy with chicken and beans. If preferred, top with crisp fried shallots and a drizzle of freshly squeezed calamansi lime.

Serves 4
Preparation time: **20 mins**
Cooking time: **40 mins**

Fried Noodles (Mee Goreng)

2 cakes firm white tofu
3 tablespoons oil
1 onion, thinly sliced
4 cloves garlic, chopped
100 g ($^1/_2$ cup) chicken breast, cut into thin strips
100 g ($^1/_2$ cup) prawns, peeled and deveined
1 tomato, cut into wedges
300 g (2 cups) sliced cabbage
150 g (3 cups) mustard greens or *bok choy*, cut in 4-cm (1$^1/_2$-in) pieces
450 g (1 lb) fresh wheat noodles, rinsed
2 eggs
2 to 3 tablespoons crisp fried shallots (page 5)
2 spring onion, thinly sliced
1 lime, cut in wedges

Sauce
1 tablespoon soy sauce
1 tablespoon black soy sauce
2 tablespoons tomato ketchup
1 teaspoon salt
2 teaspoons sugar

Chilli Paste
2 tablespoons oil
6 dried chillies, soaked and soften, drained and sliced
5 shallots, chopped
5 cloves garlic, peeled and chopped
1 teaspoon shrimp paste (*belachan*)

1 To make the Sauce, combine all the ingredients in a bowl and set aside.

2 To prepare Chilli Paste, combine chillies, shallots, garlic, and shrimp paste in a blender, adding some water and process until smooth. Heat the oil in a wok over medium heat and stir-fry the mixture until cooked and oil separates. Transfer to a bowl and clean wok.

3 Cut tofu into halves and drain on paper towels. Heat oil in a wok over medium heat and fry tofu until lightly browned on both sides. Remove from heat, place tofu on paper towels, and when cool enough to handle, cut into $^1/_2$-cm ($^1/_4$-in) thick slices. Leave remaining oil in the wok for frying the noodles.

4 Reheat the oil and stir-fry the onion and garlic for 2 minutes until fragrant. Add chicken and prawns and stir-fry for 3 minutes, then add the tomato, cabbage, and mustard greens. Increase heat to high and stir-fry for 2 minutes. Stir in the chilli paste and tofu and cook for 2 minutes more. Pour in Sauce mixture and noodles and stir-fry over high heat for 3 to 4 minutes.

5 Spread the noodles evenly over the pan. Make a well in the centre of the noodles and drizzle in 2 teaspoons oil. Add 2 eggs, stirring to scramble. Stir-fry eggs and let eggs set and brown slightly. Combine all ingredients together and serve, garnished with fried shallots and spring onions. Squeeze lime juice over noodles before eating.

Mee goreng *is best fried when cooked in small batches. With a more manageable quantity in the wok, stir-frying to the correct degree of doneness is much easier to achieve and over-cooking avoided. It is suggested that the ingredients in this recipe be divided into two, roughly equal halves and the frying done twice.*

Serves 4
Preparation time: 20 mins
Cooking time: 20–30 mins

Spicy Fried Rice Vermicelli (Mee Siam)

2 litres (8 cups) water
1 teaspoon salt
250 g (8 oz) dried rice
  vermicelli (*meehoon*)
2 eggs
Salt and freshly ground
  black pepper to taste
4 tablespoons oil
2 cakes firm white tofu
300 g (10 oz) fresh
  prawns
200 g (1 cup) chicken
  breast, cut into thin
  strips
330 g (12 oz) bean
  sprouts
200 g (3 cups) Chinese
  chives, cut in 2$^1/_2$-cm
  (1-in) lengths
1 tablespoon sugar

Seasoning Paste
3 fresh red chillies,
  chopped
5 cloves garlic
5 shallots
1 tablespoon fermented
  soy bean paste (*tau
  cheo*)

Garnish
3 tablespoons crisp fried
  shallots (see page 5)
2 spring onions (scal-
  lions), sliced
3 limes, halved

1 To make the Seasoning Paste, place chillies, garlic, shallots, and soy bean paste (*tau cheo*) in a blender, adding some water if necessary. Process until almost smooth and set aside.

2 Bring water and salt to a boil in a large pan. Add the rice vermicelli and cook until just tender, 2 to 3 minutes. Drain and set aside to cool.

3 Beat the eggs with a pinch of salt and pepper. Heat 1 teaspoon of the oil in a pan and add eggs. Working quickly, swirl the pan to allow the eggs to coat the pan, making a thin omelette. When the omelette is lightly browned, flip and cook on the other side. Fold omelette and remove from pan. Slice thinly and set aside.

4 Cut tofu into halves and drain on paper towels. Heat remaining oil in the wok and fry tofu until lightly browned on both sides. Remove to a plate and cool before cutting into $^1/_2$-cm ($^1/_4$-in) slices.

5 Over medium heat, fry the Seasoning Paste in the oil until well cooked and oil separates. Add the prawns and chicken, stir-frying until firm and cooked. Add the tofu, 1 teaspoon salt, sugar and stir-fry for 3 more minutes.

6 Add the noodles and stir-fry for 5 minutes or until the paste has spread evenly. Add the bean sprouts and chives. Cook until the vegetables are wilted but still crunchy, about 5 minutes. Taste and adjust seasoning if necessary, adding a little light soy sauce if noodles taste bland.

7 Transfer noodles onto a serving platter and garnish with the omelette strips, fried shallots, spring onions, and lime wedges. Serve immediately.

Serves 4
Preparation time: **30 mins**
Cooking time: **30 mins**

Penang Fried Kway Teow

5 tablespoons oil
1 tablespoon chopped
  garlic
250 g (8 oz) fresh
  medium prawns,
  peeled and deveined
500 g (1 lb) fresh flat rice
  noodles (*kway teow*)
250 g (4 cups) bean
  sprouts, rinsed and
  trimmed
150 g ($^3/_4$ cup) garlic
  chives cut into 5-cm
  (2-in) lengths
4 eggs
1 teaspoon salt
$^1/_4$ teaspoon freshly
  ground black pepper

Chilli Paste
8 dried chillies soaked
  and drained, sliced
1 teaspoon shrimp paste,
  crumbled

Sauce
1 tablespoon soy sauce
1 tablespoon black soy
  sauce
1 teaspoon sugar
1 tablespoon water

Serves 4
Preparation time: **20 mins**
Cooking time: **20–30 mins**

1 Combine all the Sauce ingredients and set aside.
2 To make the Chilli Paste, process or grind the chillies and shrimp paste, adding a little water if necessary.
Heat 3 tablespoons of the oil in a wok over low heat and fry the chilli paste until well cooked and the oil separates. Set the paste aside and clean the wok.
3 Heat 1 tablespoon oil and fry half the chopped garlic until golden brown. Add half the chilli paste and prawns, frying over high heat until the prawns are seared. Add half the noodles and prepared Sauce. Toss over high heat for a few minutes before spreading the noodles evenly over the wok.
4 Make a well in the centre, drizzle in a teaspoon of oil, then crack 2 eggs into it. Scramble the eggs, then combine with the noodles. Add half the bean sprouts and chives, season with the salt and ground pepper.
Stir-fry over high heat just long enough to wilt the vegetables but retain their crispness—about 1 minute.
Divide between 2 serving plates.
5 Clean pan with paper towels and repeat with the remaining half of the ingredients.

Cantonese Fried Noodles

125 ml ($^1/_2$ cup) oil
100 g ($3^1/_2$ oz) dried rice vermicelli (*meehoon*), broken into small pieces
375 g (12 oz) fresh flat rice noodles (*kway teow*)
2 tablespoons soy sauce
2 cloves garlic, chopped
5 thin slices ginger
60 g ($^1/_2$ cup) thinly sliced carrots
250 g (8 oz) chicken breast, thinly sliced
250 g (8 oz) medium prawns, peeled and deveined
150 g (5 oz) fresh squid, sliced into strips
Salt and pepper to taste
200 g (4 cups) mustard greens or *bok choy*, washed and sliced
6 dried or fresh *shiitake* mushrooms (if using dried mushrooms, soak in hot water for 20 minutes), stems removed and sliced
1 litre (4 cups) Basic Chicken Stock (see page 5)
1 tablespoon oyster sauce
1 teaspoon sugar
2 tablespoons cornflour mixed with 125 ml ($^1/_2$ cup) water
1 large egg, beaten
Seasoned Sliced Chillies (see page 4)

1 Heat oil in a wok over medium heat. Place a small handful of rice vermicelli and fry for a few seconds until puffed up but still pale. Remove immediately and place onto a paper-lined colander to drain the oil. Fry all the vermicelli this way and set aside.

2 Remove all but 3 tablespoons of oil from the wok. Reheat oil and fry the rice noodles over high heat for 3 to 4 minutes. Drizzle in 1 tablespoon of the light soy sauce. To serve, divide the noodles and vermicelli into four portions, placing them in individual plates or bowls.

3 Heat 2 tablespoons oil in a large saucepan and fry the garlic and ginger until golden brown. Add the sliced carrots, chicken, prawns and squids, stir-frying quickly over high heat for 3 to 4 minutes. Season with salt and pepper. Add mustard greens and mushrooms and cook for a few minutes.

4 Pour in chicken stock and season with oyster sauce, the remaining soy sauce and sugar. Thicken by stirring in the cornflour mixture. Slowly pour in the beaten egg, allowing the mixture to bubble and cook undisturbed for 2 to 3 minutes. Remove from the heat.

5 Ladle a generous portion of gravy over the noodles and serve immediately with Seasoned Sliced Chillies.

Serves 4
Preparation time: **30 mins**
Cooking time: **20 min**
Simmering (for stock): **1 hour**

Black Hokkien Noodles

500 g (1 lb) fresh or dried wheat noodles or fresh Japanese *udon* noodles
3 tablespoons oil
5 cloves garlic, chopped
150 g ($^3/_4$ cup) thinly sliced chicken breast
150 g (5 oz) medium prawns, peeled and deveined
150 g ($^1/_2$ cup) fresh squid, cut into $2^1/_2$-cm (1-in) pieces
3 cups mustard greens or *bok choy*, slices
1 cup round or Chinese cabbage, slices

Sauce
$2^1/_2$ tablespoons black soy sauce
1 tablespoon light soy sauce
1 tablespoon oyster sauce
2 teaspoons sugar
$^1/_2$ teaspoon salt
$^1/_4$ teaspoon ground pepper
2 teaspoons cornflour
250 ml (1 cup) water

Serves 4
Preparation time: **30 mins**
Cooking time: **20 mins**

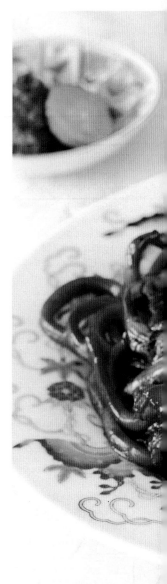

1 Mix all the Sauce ingredients together in a bowl and set aside. Bring $1^1/_2$ litres (6 cups) water to a boil in a pan. Add the noodles, let the water boil again and cook for 3 to 4 minutes or until the noodles are tender. Drain, rinse in cold water, and drain in a colander.
2 Heat oil in a wok over high heat and stir-fry the garlic until golden brown. Add the chicken and prawns and stir-fry for 2 minutes before adding the squid. Cook for 1 to 2 minutes. Pour in the sauce and bring to a boil. Add the noodles and cook for 5 to 7 minutes. Add the vegetables and stir-fry for 2 to 3 minutes. Remove from the heat and serve.
3 Prepare the fragrant shrimp paste dip (see page 5) and serve in small saucers to accompany the noodles.

Hainanese Fried Noodles

2 tablespoons oil
4 cloves garlic, chopped
100 g (4 oz) chicken
  breast, thinly sliced
100 g (4 oz) medium
  prawns, peeled and
  deveined
100 g ($^1/_4$ oz) fish cakes
  or fish fillets or dried
  tofu, thinly sliced
200 g (4 cups) mustard
  greens or *bok choy*, cut
  in 5-cm (2-in) lengths
500 g (1 lb) fresh yellow
  wheat noodles or 300 g
  (10 oz) dried wheat
  noodles, soaked in hot
  water for 20 minutes
  and drained
3 tablespoons crispy fried
  shallots (see page 5)
3 fresh red chillies or 10
  bird's eye chillies, thinly
  sliced

Gravy
1 tablespoon soy sauce
$^1/_2$ tablespoon black soy
  sauce
$^1/_2$ tablespoon oyster
  sauce
1 teaspoon sugar
$^1/_2$ teaspoon salt
$^1/_4$ teaspoon freshly
  ground pepper
200 ml ($^3/_4$ cup) water

Serves 4
Preparation time: **20 mins**
Cooking time: **20 mins**

1 To make the Gravy, combine all the gravy ingredients and set aside.
2 Heat the oil in a wok over high heat and stir-fry the garlic until golden brown. Add the chicken slices and stir-fry, then add the prawns and fish cakes (or fish fillets or tofu).
Stir-fry for 3 minutes and add the greens. Toss until wilted, about 2 minutes.
3 Pour in the Gravy mixture, bring to a boil and add the noodles. Reduce heat to medium and cook for 3 to 5 minutes. Remove from the heat and transfer to a serving platter or four individual serving plates. Garnish with fried shallots and serve immediately with sliced chillies on the side.

Coconut Rice (Nasi Lemak)

At its most basic, *nasi lemak* is a simple breakfast dish. However, with the addition of other dishes such as fried chicken, beef rendang, tamarind fried prawns, prawn sambal and cuttlefish sambal, it can be elevated to an elaborate feast.

400 g (2 cups) rice
125 ml ($^1/_2$ cup) thick
  coconut milk
425 ml ($1^3/_4$ cups)
  water
$^1/_2$ teaspoon salt
3 slices ginger
1 pandan leaf, tied into
  a knot

Serves 4
Preparation time: **15 mins**
Cooking time: **30 mins**

1 Wash rice thoroughly. Place rice in a rice cooker or heavy based saucepan and add the coconut milk, water, salt, ginger and pandan leaf.

2 If using a rice cooker, cover pan and cook according to the manufacturer's instructions. If cooking rice on a stove top, cook uncovered until all liquid has been absorbed. Stir once, cover pan with a tight-fitting lid and reduce heat to its lowest possible setting. Cook undisturbed for 20 minutes. Fluff rice up with a fork.

3 Serve with prawn sambal (see recipe below), halved hard-boiled eggs, sliced cucumbers, crisply fried dried whitebait (*ikan bilis*) and fried peanuts.

Prawn Sambal

400 g (2 cups) medium-
  sized fresh prawns
12 dried chillies, cut in
  2-cm ($^3/_4$-in) lengths
4 fresh red chillies, cut in
  2-cm ($^3/_4$-in) lengths
10 shallots, peeled and
  roughly sliced
1 teaspoon crumbled
  shrimp paste (*belachan*)
1 rounded teaspoon
  tamarind pulp
5 tablespoons oil
125 ml ($^1/_2$ cup) water
2–3 teaspoons sugar
1 teaspoon salt

Serves 4
Preparation time: **10 mins**
Cooking time: **10 mins**

1 Shell prawns and remove sand tracts. Rinse and drain in a colander.

2 Soak dried chillies in warm water until soft and plump, drain and rinse well. In a blender grind dried and fresh chillies, shallots and shrimp paste until fine, adding enough water to allow the blades to work.

3 Meanwhile, squeeze the tamarind pulp in the water, stir and strain. Discard seeds.

4 Heat oil in a wok and fry the chilli paste over low heat until well-cooked and oil separates.

5 Add prawns and fry for 5 minutes in the paste until prawns are firm and cooked. Add the tamarind juice, sugar and salt to taste. Cook for another 5 minutes, taste and adjust seasonings, then remove pan from heat.

To make a whitebait sambal (sambal ikan bilis), substitute the prawns with 100 g (3^1/2 oz) dried whitebait (ikan bilis). First remove heads and guts of fish, then fry in 6 tablespoons oil until lightly browned before draining on paper towels. Discard oil in pan. Proceed with the recipe above, adding the fish to the chilli in place of the prawns.

Claypot Chicken Rice

Traditionally, this dish is cooked and served in a claypot. If you do not own one, cooking it in a regular saucepan or rice cooker works fine.

500 g (1 lb) chicken, skinned and cut into bite-sized chunks
3 cm (1¼ in) ginger
1 tablespoon light soy sauce
1 tablespoon dark soy sauce
1 tablespoon oyster sauce
2 teaspoons sesame oil
1 teaspoon salt
¹/₂ teaspoon ground black or white pepper
1 tablespoon sugar
400 g (2 cups) long-grain rice
550 ml (2¹/₄ cups) water
2 tablespoons cooking oil

Garnish

3 tablespoons crisp fried shallots
3 tablespoons finely-sliced spring onion (scallions)
3 tablespoons fresh coriander (cilantro), optional

1 Place the chicken in a large bowl. Grate or pound the ginger and squeeze to extract juice, discarding the pulp. Marinate chicken with ginger juice, light and dark soy sauces, oyster sauce, sesame oil, salt, pepper and sugar. Set aside for 20 to 30 minutes.

2 Wash the rice thoroughly. Place rice in a roomy pan with 550 ml (2¹/₄ cups) water. Bring to a boil and cook over medium heat until almost all the water has been absorbed, about 15 minutes.

3 Place marinated chicken on top of the rice and drizzle in 2 tablespoons of cooking oil. Cover pan with a tight-fitting lid and set heat on low. Cook, undisturbed for 20 minutes, resisting the temptation to lift the lid as heat will be lost and the chicken will not cook through.

4 Flake rice, cover pan and let rice cook for another 15 minutes. Remove pan from heat. Transfer rice to a serving dish and scatter the fried shallots, spring onion and coriander leaves on top. Serve immediately, accompanied by seasoned sliced chillies (see page 4).

Serves 4
Preparation time: **30 mins**
Cooking time: **50 mins**

Place the marinated chicken on top of the rice and drizzle in the oil.

After the chicken rice has been cooking undisturbed for 20 minutes, flake the rice.

Hainanese Roast Chicken Rice

1 whole chicken (about
1^1/$_2$ kg/3 lbs)
1 tablespoon ginger juice
(from grated ginger)
1 tablespoon soy sauce
2 teaspoons honey
1 teaspoon salt
^{1}/$_2$ teaspoon ground
white pepper
^{1}/$_2$ teaspoon five spice
powder
1–2 baby cucumbers,
thickly sliced, to garnish
2 sprigs coriander leaves
(cilantro), to garnish
Chicken Rice Chilli Sauce,
to serve (see page 4)

Rice
400 g (2 cups) uncooked
long grain rice
1^1/$_2$ tablespoons oil
5 slices peeled ginger
2 tablespoons finely
minced garlic
^{1}/$_2$ teaspoon salt
600 ml (2^1/$_3$ cups)
Chicken Stock (see
page 5)

Soup
375 ml (1^1/$_2$ cups)
Chicken Stock (see
page 5)
150 g (2 cups) water-
cress or thinly sliced
Chinese cabbage
^{1}/$_2$ teaspoon salt
^{1}/$_4$ teaspoon pepper

1 Trim off the neck and fat from the chicken, then rinse and pat dry with paper towels. Combine the ginger juice, soy sauce, honey, salt, pepper and five spice powder, then rub the mixture all over the chicken (inside and out). Set aside for 20–30 minutes. Preheat oven to 200°C (400°F).

2 Place chicken in a roasting pan and roast in the pre-heated oven for 40–60 minutes (depending on size of the bird). After the first 20 minutes, reduce the heat to 170°C (350°F). Roast until the chicken skin is browned and crisp. The chicken is done if the juices run clear, not bloody, when the thigh is pierced with a fork. Remove the chicken from the oven and set aside for 15 minutes before cutting into serving portions.

3 While chicken is roasting, cook the rice. Rinse rice, then drain well. Heat the oil in a rice cooker pot or heavy-based saucepan. Fry the ginger slices and chopped garlic until golden brown. Add the rice and stir-fry for 3–4 minutes until the grains are well-coated with oil. Add the salt and chicken stock (reduce the quantity slightly if you like your rice dry).

5 Cook the Rice in a rice cooker or saucepan, uncov-ered, until the liquid level is just below the level of the rice, about 15 minutes. Cover the pan with a tight-fitting lid and cook over very low heat for a further 20 minutes. Fluff the rice up with a fork and remove the pan from the heat.

6 While rice is cooking, prepare the Soup. Rinse the watercress or cabbage, removing any bruised parts. Tear the watercress into lengths or cut the Chinese cabbage. Heat the chicken stock in a pot and add the vegetables. Cook 2–3 minutes until just soft. Season with the salt and pepper.

7 Line a serving platter with cucumber slices and arrange the chicken pieces neatly on top. Garnish with coriander leaves. Drizzle any juices left in the roasting pan over the chicken and serve with separate bowls of hot soup, rice and Chicken Rice Chilli sauce (page 4).

Serves 6
Preparation time: **40 mins**
Cooking time: **1^1/$_2$ hours**

Crispy Pancake with Lentil Curry
(Roti Canai with Dhall)

Roti Canai is a delicious crispy dough pancake and a favourite Malaysian breakfast dish which may also be eaten throughout the day. Roti Canai may be accompanied by virtually any meat or vegetable curry. The recipe for Roti Canai is on page 48.

Lentil Curry (Dhall)

100 g ($^1/_2$ cup) split chickpeas (*channa dal*), washed
900 ml ($3^1/_2$ cups) water
$^1/_4$ teaspoon ground turmeric
1 medium onion, chopped
1 small carrot, sliced
1 small round eggplant, chopped
1 medium tomato, cut into wedges
2 green chillies, cut into 2-cm ($^3/_4$-in) lengths
1 heaped teaspoon tamarind pulp
125 ml ($^1/_2$ cup) warm water
100 ml (scant $^1/_2$ cup) thin coconut milk or plain milk
Salt to taste
3 tablespoons oil
$^1/_2$ teaspoon black mustard seeds
$^1/_2$ teaspoon cumin seeds
1 sprig curry leaves
1 dried red chilli, cut into 2-cm ($^3/_4$-in) lengths
3 shallots, thinly sliced
3 cloves garlic, thinly sliced

1 Remove any grit from lentils and put in a saucepan with water and turmeric. Bring to a boil over high heat. Reduce heat to low and simmer for 20 minutes.
2 Add onion, carrot, aubergine, and tomato. Cook for another 20 minutes, or until vegetables are tender. Add the green chillies during the last 5 minutes of cooking.
3 Soak the tamarind pulp in warm water for 5 minutes. Squeeze and strain to obtain the juice. Add the coconut milk, salt, and tamarind juice. Cook for 5 minutes and remove pan from heat.
4 Meanwhile, heat the oil in a wok over medium heat. Fry mustard and cumin seeds for 30 seconds or until they pop. Add curry leaves, dried chillies, shallots, and garlic. Fry until shallots and garlic turn golden brown. Spoon into the pea mixture, stir well, cover pan, and remove from the heat.

Serves 4
Preparation time: 30 mins
Cooking time: 50 mins

Crispy Pancake (Roti Canai)

Roti Canai is a delicious crispy pancake and a favourite Malaysian dish, enjoyed and eaten throughout the day. This is an unconventional way to make Roti Canai , but it is an easier method for the home cook to follow than attempting to duplicate the skilled manoeuvres of a Roti Canai cook.

$^1/_2$ tablespoon oil for frying

Dough 1
360 g (3 cups) plain flour
1$^1/_2$ teaspoons salt
1 tablespoon sugar
30 g (4 tablespoons) softened butter or oil
1 egg, beaten
125 ml ($^1/_2$ cup) milk
5 tablespoons water

Dough 2
180 g (1$^1/_2$ cups) plain flour
130 g ($^1/_2$ cup) softened butter or oil

Makes 16 pancakes
Preparation time: **30 mins**
Standing time: **1–2 hours**
Cooking time: **20 mins**

1 To make Dough 1, combine flour, salt, and sugar in a mixing bowl. Add in the softened butter or oil. Beat egg and milk together in a measuring cup and add enough water to make 250 ml (1 cup) of liquid.

2 Mix the softened butter or oil into the flour mixture well using your fingertips. Add 180 ml ($^3/_4$ cup) of the egg-milk mixture slowly. Mix by hand to make a fairly soft, pliable dough. If dough seems dry, add remaining liquid a bit at a time. Once the dough starts to bind, stop adding liquid.

3 Knead well on a lightly floured surface for 10 to 15 minutes, until the dough is smooth and elastic.

4 Form into a thick roll and divide into 8 equal pieces with a knife.

5 Roll each piece of dough into a smooth balls. Coat generously with softened butter or oil. set aside for 1 to 2 hours. To make Dough 2, combine flour and butter or oil in a bowl and mix with a fork until the mixture forms a soft, smooth dough. Divide into 8 pieces and roll each into a ball. Cover with a clean cloth and set aside.

6 To make a pancake, flatten one Dough 1 ball into a disk about 7 cm (3 in) in diameter. Place one Dough 2 ball on top and wrap the flat disk up and around the ball.

7 On a lightly floured surface, use a rolling pin to roll the ball into a rectangular sheet mea suring 13 x 16 cm (5 x 6 $^1/_2$ in).

8 Roll the dough up length wise.

9 Flatten the roll into a thin sheet again. Now roll it up from the short end to make a short, fat roll.

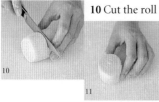

10 Cut the roll into 2 equal halves.

11 Sit the dough on its side, then roll each piece out thinly with a rolling pin. You will get a thin disk of dough lightly marked with concentric circles which will fry up into a light, flaky pancakes.

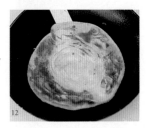

12 Heat $^1/_2$ tablespoon oil on a griddle and cook the Roti Canai over medium heat for 2 to 3 minutes on each side or until golden brown. When done, transfer to a flat surface and, using cupped hands, press the Roti Canai from the outside towards the centre to fluff the layers. Serve hot with Lentil Curry (see page 46).

Crispy Egg Pancake (Roti Telur)

One portion of Roti
Canai doughs 1 and 2
2 eggs
2 tablespoons chopped
onion
Salt and pepper to taste
Oil for frying

Makes 16 pancakes
Preparation time: 40 mins
Standing time: 1–2 hours
Cooking time: 20 mins

1 Shape the dough according to the instructions for Roti Canai (up to step 11), but roll out the dough into slightly thinner circles, approximately 17 cm (7 in) across.

2 Crack an egg into a small bowl and beat with a fork—just to break up the yolk—do not overbeat. Pour the beaten egg onto the centre of the pastry circle; try not to let the egg run over the edge of the pastry. Scatter a spoonful of chopped onion over the egg and season with a pinch of salt and pepper.

3 Carefully fold the circle over to enclose the egg, and press down the edge to seal it. The final shape will be a semi-circle.

4 Heat half a tablespoon of oil on a griddle or heavy based frying pan over medium heat. Carefully lift the *roti telur* onto the hot pan and cook on medium heat for 2 to 3 minutes on each side or until puffed up and golden brown. Serve hot with any kind of curry.

Roti telur *is just one of many variations of* roti canai. *Other delicious possibilities are* roti planta *(butter pancake),* roti bawang *(onion pancake),* roti sardin *(sardine pancake),* roti aiskrim *(ice-cream pancake) and* roti bom *(crsipy pancake exploded between cupped hands). Experiment using the filling of your choice.*

Pour the beaten egg into the centre of the pastry circle then add the onion.

Fold the pastry into a semi-circle and fry on each side until golden brown.

Stuffed Pancake (Murtabak)

Dough

200 g (1¹/₂ cups) plain flour
¹/₂ teaspoon salt
2 teaspoons sugar
2 tablespoons softened butter or margarine
125 ml (¹/₂ cup) milk

Filling

2 tablespoons oil
4 onions, diced into ¹/₂-cm (¹/₄-in) cubes
2 cm (³/₄ in) ginger, finely chopped
300 g (1¹/₂ cups) lean minced mutton, beef or chicken
2 tablespoons ground cumin
¹/₂ tablespoon chilli powder
¹/₂ tablespoon garam masala
¹/₄ teaspoon ground black pepper
1 level teaspoon salt
3 tablespoons roughly chopped celery leaves or fresh coriander
1 green chilli, finely chopped
5 eggs, beaten

Makes 5 pancakes
Preparation time: 30 mins
Standing time: 1–2 hours
Cooking time: 20 mins

1 Combine flour, salt and sugar in a mixing bowl. Mix in the softened butter with your fingertips until well distributed. Pour in milk and mix with your hands to make a soft, pliable dough. Knead well on a lightly floured surface until dough is smooth and elastic, about 10 minutes.

2 Form dough into a thick sausage shape and divide into 5 equal pieces. Roll into smooth balls, coating each one generously with oil, and place in a bowl. Cover with a clean cloth and set aside for 1 to 2 hours (this resting time is crucial as it makes the dough more elastic and easy to stretch).

3 While the dough rests, make the filling. Heat oil in a frying pan and soften ginger and half the onion over medium heat. Add the minced meat, spices and seasonings, stir-frying it well until meat is browned and spices smell fragrant. Remove pan from heat and transfer filling to a large, shallow dish. Stir in remaining diced onion, chopped coriander or celery leaves and green chilli. Spread filling out and allow to cool.

4 To shape *murtabak*, lightly drizzle a clean tabletop or countertop with oil. Place a ball of dough on it and flatten it evenly with your palms. Carefully stretch the dough, working around the circle until it is very thinly stretched to about 30 cm (12 in) in diameter.

5 Divide the filling into five roughly equal portions. For every *murtabak*, place one portion of filling into a bowl and break in one egg. Beat with a fork to mix well and place this mixture in the centre of the stretched circle of dough, spreading it out into a square, roughly 13 x 13 cm (5 x 5 in). Fold the dough over the filling to enclose the filling in a neat square.

6 Heat a heavy-based frying pan or griddle over low heat and drizzle in a tablespoonful of oil. Transfer the *murtabak* to the pan, being careful not to make any tears. Cook over low heat for 3 to 4 minutes on either side or until *murtabak* is golden brown on the outside and the inside is cooked through. Serve with pink pickled onion (see page 4).

Place filling in the centre of the stretched circle of dough then fold the sides in.

Wrap the murtabak neatly as you would a square or rectangular parcel.

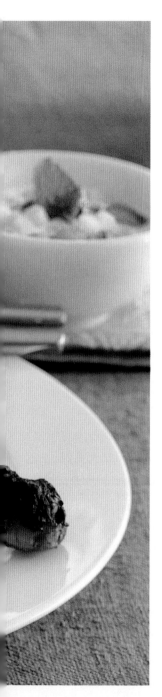

Tandoori Chicken & Naan

Tandoori chicken is traditionally roasted in a special clay oven, but in a domestic kitchen the closest and easiest way to imitate this is to cook it under an electric or gas grill. The recipe for *naan* bread is on page 56.

	Marinade
4 whole chicken legs, about 275 g (9 oz) each	6 cloves garlic
Lime wedges	4 cm (1 1/2 in) ginger
1/2 onion, thinly sliced	4 teaspoons chilli powder
	4 teaspoons garam masala
Serves 4	2 teaspoons salt
Preparation time: 20 mins	2 tablespoons lime juice
Standing time: 2–3 hours	4 tablespoons yoghurt
Cooking time: 20–30 mins	3 tablespoons oil

1 Remove skin and visible fat from chicken legs and make a few diagonal cuts on the thicker parts to allow for even cooking and for marinade to penetrate.
2 To prepare marinade, pound garlic and ginger finely in a mortar and pestle or grate finely. Combine this with the chilli powder, garam masala, salt, lime juice, yoghurt and oil. Coat the chicken pieces with this mixture, ensuring that they are well covered with the marinade. Transfer the chicken into a clean, roomy plastic bag where the marinade can coat the meat more efficiently. Squeeze excess air out, seal and refrigerate for 2 to 3 hours.
3 Preheat grill to high. Arrange chicken on a wire rack, leaving a little space in between each piece and grill fairly close to the source of heat. Cook for 10 minutes on each side or until chicken is well browned and cooked through. (Test by inserting a skewer or tip of a knife into the thigh—the juices should not be pink or tinged with blood.)
4 Serve hot with rice or *naan* (recipe on page 56). Traditionally, wedges of lime and thinly sliced raw onion are served with the chicken. Squeeze a little lime juice on the chicken for added tang.

Leavened Bread (Naan)

Naan is traditionally baked plastered to the side of a clay tandoor oven and peeled off when done. In a domestic kitchen, good results can also be obtained by cooking it in a frying pan.

1 teaspoon white vinegar
50 ml (scant $^1/_4$ cup) full cream milk (fresh or UHT)
1 teaspoon sugar
100 ml (scant $^1/_2$ cup) water (at room temperature)
1$^1/_2$ teaspoons instant yeast granules
360 g (3 cups) plain flour
1 teaspoon salt
100 ml (scant $^1/_2$ cup) water

Makes 8 naan
Preparation time: **30 mins**
Standing time: **2 hours**
Cooking time: **40 mins**

Stir the vinegar into the milk and set aside until the mixture curdles and thickens, about 15 minutes. Stir the sugar into the first 100 ml (scant $^1/_2$ cup) water and sprinkle in the yeast. Stir to dissolve and set aside until frothy, about 15 minutes (see left).

Place flour and salt into a mixing bowl, hollow out a well in the centre. Pour in yeast liquid, soured milk and water and mix with your hands to get a fairly soft dough. If dough seems too wet and sticky, dust in an extra tablespoon of flour.

Knead well on a lightly floured surface until dough feels smooth and elastic, about 10 to 15 minutes.

Place dough in a lightly oiled mixing bowl and cover with damp cloth. Leave to rise until doubled in bulk, about 1 hour.

Knead dough, roll into a thick sausage shape and divide into 8 roughly equal pieces. Roll each piece into a smooth ball and leave to rise on a lightly floured surface until well risen and light, about 30 minutes.

Dust your working surface lightly with flour and using your fingers, flatten the balls into ovals slightly larger than your palm—they should be about $1/2$ cm ($1/4$ in) thick. Lay them on a well-floured surface, cover with a clean, dry cloth and leave to rise until dough feels spongy and light to the touch, about 20 minutes more.

Heat a heavy-based frying pan (preferably one with a lid) over high heat and cook one *naan* at a time on the ungreased surface for about 2 minutes per side, keeping the lid on while the bread is cooking. Serve immediately with curry or tandoori chicken.

If not eating immediately, *naan* can be cooled on a wire tray and stored in a clean, dry polythene bag, where it can keep for 2 days in the refrigerator or 2 weeks in the freezer. To reheat, sprinkle lightly with water and cook for 1 to 2 minutes on each side, in a frying pan. (Frozen *naan* should be left to thaw at room temperature before reheating.)

Iced Barley

100 g (½ cup) pearl
  barley
4 litres (16 cups) water
2 pandan leaves
Sugar to taste
Ice cubes

Serves 4
Preparation time: **10 mins**
Cooking time: **50 mins**

1 Wash barley in several changes of water until water runs clear. Place in a roomy saucepan with 4 litres water. Bring water to a boil and cook barley on medium heat until barley grains have bloomed and softened, about 30 to 40 minutes. (Do not boil for longer than an hour as overcooked barley will produce a slimy, cloudy drink.)

2 Towards the last 10 minutes of boiling, add the pandan leaves and enough sugar to sweeten to taste. Cool barley thoroughly and serve in tall glasses with plenty of ice.

Soya Bean Milk

150 g (5 oz) dried soya beans
1 1/2 litres (6 cups) water
2 pandan leaves
Sugar to taste

Serves 4
Soaking time: overnight
Preparation time: 30 mins
Cooking time: 20 mins

1 Rinse soya beans in several changes of water. Cover with fresh water and soak overnight. The next day, rinse beans and remove any loose skins floating around in the water. Drain beans and, working in small batches at a time, place beans in the jug of a blender, adding enough water to enable the blades to work. Whisk beans until smooth and fine.

2 Pass beans through a very fine sieve or place in a muslin bag and squeeze until dry. To obtain the maximum amount of soya bean extract, process the beans in the blender a second time round, using the water from the 1 1/2 litres specified.

3 Pour the strained soya bean milk into a roomy saucepan and bring to a boil over gentle heat. Add the knotted pandan leaves and simmer for 15 minutes. Sweeten to taste and take the pan off the heat. Cool thoroughly and chill milk in the fridge. Soya bean milk may be served with ice. Drink within 24 hours of making.

Shaved Ice with Red Beans (Ice Kacang)

You really need an ice-shaving machine to make this dessert properly, but if you do not have one, you can put ice cubes in a blender, although this will make it more like a drink than the dessert that it is. Although not widely available, cooked, sweetened red kidney beans can be bought in tins. If you are unable to obtain them, you can make them from scratch.

200 g (1 cup) red kidney or azuki beans
Sugar to taste
200 g (1 cup) seaweed jelly, finely chopped
300 g (1 cup) creamed corn
250 ml (1 cup) evaporated milk
150 ml ($^2/_3$ cup) fruit-flavoured or rose syrup
150 ml ($^2/_3$ cup) brown sugar, palm sugar, or maple syrup
Freshly shaved ice or crushed ice cubes

Serves 4
Preparation time: **10 mins**
Assembling time: **10 mins**

1 Rinse beans and soak until plump (soak kidney beans overnight, adzuki beans for 1 to 2 hours). Rinse beans and cover with 1 litre (4 cups) fresh water. Bring beans and water to boil in a large pan and cook until beans are tender. (They should be soft but still hold their shape, about 40 minutes for the small adzuki beans and $1^1/_2$ hours for the larger kidney beans). Sweeten to taste. Set aside to cool.

2 To serve, place a generous spoonful of beans, seaweed jelly, and corn in a deep serving bowl. Top with a mound of shaved ice and drizzle in a spoonful each of fruit and brown sugar syrups. Pour on 1 to 2 tablespoons of evaporated milk and serve immediately.

Palm sugar syrup *can be made by chopping up chunks of the palm sugar and adding a little water, cooking over low heat until it caramelizes.*

Sweet Coconut Milk Pudding (Chendol)

Shaved ice or ice cubes
  to serve
375 ml (1 1/2 cups) thick
  coconut milk

Palm Sugar Syrup
150 ml (2/3 cup) water
200 g (1 1/4 cups)
  coarsely chopped palm
  sugar

Pandan Extract
10 pandan leaves
200 ml (3/4 cup) water

Chendol Jellies
6 tablespoons green pea
  flour
2 tablespoons rice flour

Serves 4
Preparation time: **40 mins**
Cooking time: **20 min**

1 To make the pandan extract, wash the pandan leaves and cut into 2-cm (3/4-in) lengths. Place in a blender with 200 ml (3/4 cup) water and grind until the leaves become liquidised. Strain through a sieve and squeeze the pulp to obtain the pandan extract. Discard solids.

2 To make the chendol jellies, pour pandan extract into a measuring jug and top up with water to make up a total of 500 ml (2 cups) liquid. Add the green pea flour and rice flour. Stir well until free from lumps then strain this mixture into a pan. Cook over medium heat, stirring continuously, until mixture boils and thickens, about 5 minutes.

3 Remove pan from heat and form the chendol jellies into little strands (see note). If using a perforated ladle, hold above a bowl containing iced water and, working with a spoonful of dough at a time, pass it through the holes in the ladle by pressing on the mixture with a spoon or rubber spatula. The dough should pass through in little strands. Remember to work fairly quickly, as you must shape the chendol jellies while the mixture is still very warm. Once it cools, the mixture will set and it will become difficult to press it through the perforations.

4 To make the palm sugar syrup, place the water and palm sugar in a saucepan. Bring to a boil and simmer over medium heat until the sugar dissolves and the mixture becomes syrupy. Set aside to cool then strain into a jug or bowl.

5 To serve , place 2–3 tablespoons of the chendol jellies in a bowl and top with a plenty of shaved ice (or 5–6 ice cubes). Pour in 125 ml (1/2 cup) thick coconut milk and drizzle on 1–2 spoonfuls of palm sugar syrup to sweeten. Serve immediately.

Traditionally, the cooked chendol *mixture is passed through a frame with round holes, but if you don't own a chendol-making frame, you can improvise by using a perforated ladle. The above recipe will produce chendol of a natural, muted shade of green. If you prefer a brighter-coloured chendol, add 2 drops of green colouring to the mixture before you cook it.*

Index